God Encounters are Real

By LaVerne Moore-Slaughter

© 2019 LaVerne Moore-Slaughter

Published by:
LaVerne Moore-Slaughter

All rights reserved. No part of this book may be reproduced or transmitted in any form or by any means including, but not limited to, electronic or mechanical, photocopying, recording, or by any information storage and retrieval system without written permission from the publisher, except for the inclusion of brief quotations in review. All Scripture quotations, unless otherwise indicated, are taken from the King James Version (KJV) of the Holy Bible.

Author: LaVerne Moore-Slaughter
Cover Designer: Zoë Life Creative Team

First U.S. Edition 2019 Soft cover

Publisher's Cataloging-In-Publication Data

Moore-Slaughter, LaVerne
God Encounters are Real!

13 Digit ISBN 978-0-9995405-6-5 Soft Cover, Perfect Bind

Christian Living, Spiritual Growth, Spirituality

Printed in the United States of America

GEAR v8 7-27-2019

Dedication

This book is dedicated to my Lord and Savior, Jesus Christ, who is the head of my life. I give Him the Praise and the Honor for all He has done for me.

In memory of my parents, Earnest and Lucinda Paige, Robert (brother), Godmother Mosella Earl, and my beloved husband George R. Slaughter, all whom have gone home to be with the Lord. To my son, Raymond (Glen) Thomas, my spiritual daughter, Sabrina Adams, my adorable grandchildren, Brittany, Cole and Joy, my sisters, brothers, relatives and friends who are all precious to me.

Dr. Rosalind Griffin, Farmington Hills, Michigan, who helped me embrace myself with the understanding that I was not losing my mind, but that I was going through depression due to the loss of my mother, January 1999, the diagnosis of stomach cancer, February 1999, and the divorce from my business in May 1999. Thank God that she listened.

Acknowledgments

To my late husband George R. Slaughter, thank you for being my coach and giving me moral support all the years you were with me.

To my son, Ray G. Thomas, I thank you for your encouragement and always believing that your mom can conquer anything.

To all of my siblings: Earnestine, Cheryl, George, Charlene and Dennis for being there for one another when times were good and bad.

To my niece Artesia McNeal-Washington, for being instrumental in my later years.

To my extended family in Florida for being there for me whenever I needed them.

Endorsements

Laverne Moore is a chosen vessel with a special gift from God. Her encounter with the Savior has fostered a passion within that you can hear in her voice, see in her life, and experience in her writings. I have personally experienced her insightful wisdom from God, and it assisted me in my growth as a Christian. Laverne's life has had its share of difficulties, nevertheless, her encounter with the True and Living God has empowered her to stand and be triumphant. Thankfully, Laverne has taken the time to compile her experiences in a book that will inspire, motivate, excite, and awaken your senses so that you will develop your intimacy with God and arise to your divine calling and destiny.

—Elker L. Harris, Pastor
Mt. Calvary Missionary Baptist Church of Stuart Florida

First hand knowledge has always proven to be the most reliable when it comes to the intent and character of a person.

For over twenty-years, I have been a witness and recipient of Laverne Moore's faith, love and friendship.

Her unselfish instinct to place others needs and comfort (sometimes before her own) is just more proof of her God led life.

Let your soul be blessed by her words and wisdom that she so artfully lays out in her new book, "*God Encounters are Real*" I promise you will thank yourself for it.

—Kim Padgett
Jewelery Designer/Stylist

God Encounters are Real

Table of Contents

Special Note to the Reader... 12

Chapter 1 - Before the Beginning........................... 15
- Life Influences
- A Mother's Wisdom Shared
- Heart
- A Personal Prophecy that Revealed my Future

Chapter 2 - Introduction... 21
- Unexplainable Encounter
- Who Was in the Mirror?
- God Did it

Chapter 3 - Encounters with God at the Altar............ 25
- Mother Grace
- Samuel
- Fly Away

Chapter 4 - Vibratory Experiences........................... 29
- The Beauty Shop Back in the Day
- Who is Louise?
- Divine Design
- Special Delivery
- Sadness in the Nail Salon
- Who's Calling
- The Church Seat that was Left for Me
- Presidential Encounter

Table of Contents (continued)

Chapter 5 - Dreams.. 39
- Joanne and the White House
- He Shall Be Healed
- One Way Connection
- The Little Girl Was Rescued
- The Day
- Hope
- The Visit After Church
- Mistaken Diagnosis
- Blind
- The Math Problems That Were Solved
- Soul Mate
- The Nap I Will Never Forget
- My Own Diagnosis—Homeostasis
- Untangled
- Battling Your Way Through Life
- The Three Little Pigs

Chapter 6 - Random Acts of Kindness............................ 57
- Paying Forward
- Valentine's Day Surprise
- Tears Shared with the Parking Lot Attendant

Chapter 7 - Auditory.. 61
- Something is Going to Happen to You Today
- The Enemy
- Divorce the Business
- Around the Corner

Table of Contents (continued)

Chapter 8 - Inspired Writings.. 69
    - A Mom's Message to her Child
    - Let the Rain Fall
    - Celebrating Life
    - Around the Corner
    - A Message to my Lovely Wife
    - Listen
    - Missionary in Disguise

Chapter 9 - Poetry in the Moment.. 77
    - Inspirational Poetry

Chapter 10 - My Definitions... 85
    - The Way I Define Certain Words

Epilogue.. 88

About the Author (LaVerne Moore-Slaughter)............ 91

Special Note to the Readers

I am not a psychic. God just gives me messages to give to others from time to time. It's not something that happens on a daily basis. It's nothing planned. It just happens.

"Do not neglect the spiritual gift you received through the prophecy spoken over you when the elders of the church laid their hands on you"
(1 Timothy 4:14, NLT).

I believe everyone can have this same connection with God, all you need is to be a willing vessel and have your heart and mind aligned with the heart and mind of the Master.

Do you choose to be a willing vessel today?

1
Before the Beginning

"Your hands made me and formed me..."
James 5:14

Life Influences

My parents were born and raised in the Mississippi Delta area. They moved to Detroit, Michigan in the early 1940s with my oldest brother and sister. Ten years later, I was born followed by four more siblings.

Because my parent's education was limited, they thought graduating from high school was a big deal; so, they never talked to us about going to college. That was a decision we had to make on our own. After high school, we were expected to get a job, be responsible and take care of ourselves. My father would always remind us that he didn't have an opportunity to go to school because he had to help take care of his mother and siblings. I chose to believe he lacked the knowledge of the importance of college. My father's philosophy was: *"When you are eighteen years old, you are grown and you are on your own and nobody owes you anything."*

In today's society, my father would have been labeled a workaholic. He would go to his primary job at General Motors, come home to have dinner with the family and then take one of my brothers with him to do various plumbing jobs in the evening. He continued to do plumbing jobs until he became ill at the age of eighty-seven. He was an excellent provider, but frugal. He was known in the community as "Mr. Paige, the Plumber." He made his transition on May 20, 2003.

My Mother was a stay-at-home mom. She taught us daily living skills and made sure that we were well cared for. Although she was in an out of the hospital with severe asthma, when she was at home she would still struggle to get up and cook well-balanced meals with homemade desserts. She made sure that we sat down as a family and had dinner together. She made the neighbors feel welcome to come and eat if they were hungry. She had a lot of will power and would tell us children that you can't lie in the bed because you aren't

Before the Beginning

feeling well. If you get up and try doing something, you might feel better.

As kids, we would seldom fake having a bellyache to miss school, because my mother would make us get up anyway and do something around the house. We had to be almost dead to stay in the bed. Her famous words were, *"If I can get up sick and work around the house, so can you."*

A Mother's Wisdom Shared

I owe a lot to my mother. She instilled in her children, wisdom, values and principles. She reinforced what was right and what was expected to live a good life.

- Love your neighbor as yourself.
- Treat people the way you want to be treated.
- What you put out, you will reap.
- Lend a helping hand.
- Don't expect to receive pay for everything you do for others, God will bless you for it.
- Remember it's good to be educated, but you better have common sense to go along with it.
- Don't hold a grudge.
- Learn to forgive one another. If you don't, you will cut off your blessings.
- Work for what you want and have something to show for it.
- Don't try cheating your way through life.
- Remember it's nice to go to church every Sunday, but if your heart is not right, you aren't right.
- God is looking at your heart, and how you treat your fellowman.

My mother's maiden name was Collins. She was one of twelve children, the majority of them were self-made entrepreneurs, so she always knew how to generate extra income. As we grew older, she and my oldest brother bought a truck and sold watermelon and fish. Later in life, she was part-owner of a nightclub business and she also owned rental property.

My mom and her friends loved to play Keno, Bingo, and other card games. My mother's sister-in-law told me she did not allow her girls to come over to our house (Sister Cindy's) because my mom had gambling parties. I said, "Yeah…you are right, my mom taught us how to count money."

My mom had unconditional love for her children and her grandchildren. She babysat all her grandchildren and spoiled them rotten.

In 1978, she convinced my father to help one of my brothers invest in a nightclub business, Detroit Studio 54. She asked me to be their business partner. I quit my job working in the healthcare field to work in the night club business. When I began, I only knew that Gin was "white" and Whiskey was "brown." I had no knowledge of the different brands of liquor and I wasn't a nightlife person. After six years of doing something I didn't enjoy, I told God I would do what He wanted me to do, even if it meant going broke. Well guess what! That's exactly what happened—I went broke.

My mother retired from the business after becoming very upset with me for leaving the company. Eventually, she got over being upset and began to travel with her children. She enjoyed her life until her death on January 22, 1999.

Heart

Is your heart big or small?
Is your heart sweet or bitter?
Is your heart right or wrong?
The heart is your life.

A Personal Prophecy that Revealed My Future

My godmother, Moselle Gollman, was my mother's best friend, she would always say to me, "Out of seven children, I chose you to be my goddaughter." She never called me LaVerne, she called me "Yvonne."

Moselle was very inspirational to me and others. When I was ten years old, she told me I was going to work with sick people. My reply was, "How do you know that? I hate blood." She was very strange and comical.

She then said, "Listen to me little girl, God gave me a gift, and some kind of connection I can't explain, but Mother Mary communicates with me." Most people were afraid of her because they did not understand her gift. She was able to walk in a room of strangers and begin telling individuals about themselves. I can relate to her feelings, because I have had similar experiences. It's like a sixth sense. Well, her predictions of my life definitely came true. The majority of my life has been dedicated to caring for the sick and lending a helping hand, whenever I could.

2

Introduction

"Those who listen to instruction will prosper, those who trust the Lord will be joyful."
Proverbs 16:20 (NLT)

Unexplainable Encounters

Over the years, I have had several unexplainable things happen in my life. I call these happenings encounters with God. These encounters came through dreams, visions, vibratory experiences, spiritual discernment, auditory encounters and inspired writings. Few truly understand my encounters with God. Most people think it's just a coincidence when these things happen. I thank God that He has chosen me to be a blessing to others in this way—It's all about Him not all about me.

I wrote **God Encounters are Real** to share proof, based on my personal experiences, that God is real. As you turn the pages, you'll read how my encounters are founded on something much greater than coincidence. I believe we all have a subconscious connection with God.

Are you tuned in and ready to be connected?

Introduction

Who Was In the Mirror?

Early one morning when I was a kid, I woke up and saw the image of Jesus in the mirror of my old fashioned dresser. I wonder...was that the beginning of my spiritual awakening?

God Did It

God gave us the air to breathe
The wind to feel
The nose to smell
The Mouth to speak
and
The ears to hear His voice that's near.

3
Encounters with God at the Altar

Is any sick among you?
Let him call for the elders of the church;
and let them pray over him,
anointing him with oil in the name of the Lord
(James 5:14).

Mother Grace

In 1970, my mother and godmother asked me to take them to a Monday night church service. Reluctantly, I drove them. After getting there, I realized this church service was totally different from what I was accustomed to.

During the service, the minister asked everyone to stand and come to the altar for prayer or to pray for someone who needed prayer. I stood up, but did not go to the altar, I was too busy looking at the people shouting and running up and down the aisles of the church. I whispered to the lady standing next to me, "What is going on?"

She explained that this is the way that some people praise the Lord. Well, about five or ten minutes later, the minister said, "There is someone in here who doesn't quite understand what is going on, but they need to come to the altar and pray for a miracle."

Instantly, I remembered Mother Grace who was sick in the hospital with stomach cancer and in grave condition. So I made my way to the altar and began to ask God to heal Mother Grace of cancer. WOW! The next thing I knew, I was getting up off the floor. I wasn't sure how long I had been lying on the floor knocked out. Later, I was told I had been "slain in the spirit," *(a term used by Pentecostal and charismatic Christians to describe a form of prostration in which an individual falls to the floor while experiencing religious ecstasy. Believers attribute this behavior to the power of the Holy Spirit).*

The next morning, my mother received a telephone call from the hospital. She was surprised, the voice on the phone was Mother Grace's. The day before Mother Grace's doctors had called the family to come to the hospital, because they did not expect her to make it through the night. Mother

Encounters with God at the Altar

Grace lived for an additional seven years. When she did die, she died of a heart attack, not cancer. I attribute those additional years to the prayer which was prompted by Divine Intervention.

Who are you being prompted to pray for today?

Samuel

I was invited by the late Pastor J. of New Prospect Missionary Baptist Church of Detroit, to come and hear her preach while she was in Miami, Florida in May 2006.

During the church service the pastor of the church had an altar call and asked everyone to pray for someone they knew who were in need of prayer. While standing there praying for my family members, a young lady I knew came across my mind, and I began to pray for her.

She was having a difficult pregnancy and felt she was going to lose her baby. I began to pray for her and the name Samuel was revealed to my heart. The spirit was very high in the church service and I felt the anointing of the Holy Spirit. I don't claim to know everything about the Bible, so I went home after church that day and read the book of Samuel.

In 1 Samuel 1:20, it said, *"Wherefore it came to pass, when the time was come about after Hannah had conceived, that she bare a son, and called his name Samuel, [saying], Because I have asked him of the LORD."*

The following day, I called the young lady and told her about my encounter with God at church the previous day and I felt confident that everything was going to be alright with the unborn child. The mother wept and thanked me for giving her that reassurance. Later, I learned the pregnancy was going fine and she had no other problems carrying the baby. The mom had a healthy baby boy. I give God all the praise and the honor for using me to give this mom a message to help ease her mind.

Fly Away

Fly away in your mind like a bird.
Have confidence that God can carry you, like the birds.
The birds fly from place to place without a worry.
Fly above your problems.
They can never reach the sky.
They are only a few inches from the soil.
Therefore, it's plenty of room to grow between each problem that we have.
God says, turn each problem over to Me. God is majestic and attentive to our needs.
He hears all, Knows all,
And forgives all. God wants us free.

4
Vibratory Experienc-

*In Webster's dictionary, vibration is the root word of vibratory. One of the definitions listed is "a distinctive usually emotional atmosphere capable of being sensed."
I have had several vibratory experiences that have been confirmed, but these are the most profound ones.*

The Beauty Shop Back in the Day

Back in the day—1969—beauticians had their hair salons in their basements. Looking back, I can't believe I would sit there half a day to get my hair styled and listen to all the gossip and baggage the women were talking about. It was juicy! They would talk about what happened to them last night; my man dumped me for another woman and so on. That's when everybody would join the conversation and tell their story. "I wouldn't take that from him..."Everybody was giving some type of advice based upon their past experiences.

On this particular Saturday morning, I got there early so I could get out by noon. While sitting under the hair dryer, I felt a heaviness come upon me and I didn't know what was going on.

I got up and started walking around the cramped basement. The beautician yelled, "LaVerne, get back under the dryer! I have someone waiting for your seat!" Well, I got back under the hair dryer and the same thing happened again. This time, I felt the hair rise up on my arms. So, I began to rub my arms and to talk under my breath, "God, I don't like this feeling. What's going on?"

I couldn't hold my feelings any longer and felt compelled to ask a young lady that I didn't know if something was going on. I told her I was feeling strange, but couldn't explain the reason why. I went on to explain to her how I was feeling and she said she could relate to it. She said, "My mom died and I'm preparing myself for her funeral."

Vibratory Experiences

Who is Louise?

While in the healthcare business, Gwen, one of the employees ask for a ride home. So, I volunteered to give her a lift. When she got out of my car, the name Louise stayed on my mind and I did not know why. The next day when Gwen arrived at work, I asked her if she knew a Louise. She gave me this strange look and said, "Yes, that was my grandmother's name, she raised me, and I have thought about her every day since she died. How did you know her name?"

I told her when she got out of my car yesterday the name Louise came to my mind for no apparent reason. I told her that this person, Louise, was in her vibration and that was the reason I felt her presence. When I gave her some comforting words she began to cry.

I remember telling Gwen that her grandmother wanted her to focus on herself and to stop allowing people to take advantage of her and learn to save something for a rainy day. She said the words I spoke to her were the exact words that her grandmother would have said. Gwen hugged me and said that I confirmed what she had been feeling and the advice her grandmother would have given her.

Who might need your comfort today?

Divine Design

I had another encounter at a different salon. After changing my regular Wednesday hair appointment to Saturday of the same week, I ran into the hair stylist's sister,

Anna, by surprise. She had changed her hair appointment to this day as well. It was only by Divine Design that this opportunity was presented to share with Anna what God had put on my heart concerning her and her husband, Bill. I wasn't sure how I would start this conversation with her, because she was convinced that her husband had been completely healed from cancer and that he was doing fine. I didn't know him personally, I had only seen him a few times coming in and out the salon. I knew that Bill had been diagnosed with lung cancer, because I had overheard the conversation in the beauty shop.

Earlier that week I called Karen, the hair stylist, and asked her how her brother-in-law was doing and she said, "Okay." I became really confused about the message that I had received that morning.

Oftentimes, I receive messages while in the shower. I didn't understand why I received a message about someone I barely knew. But that's God's business!

Karen put me under the hair dryer and sat Anna next to me. I began to have an uncomfortable feeling and wondered if I should say anything to Anna. She appeared to be in good spirits. We were not talking, while under the noisy hair dryers, but that only lasted for a few moments. I got up enough nerve and tapped her on her leg and asked her how her husband was doing. She sad, "Bill is doing fine."

Again, this lady had unshakable faith in God and had no doubt that her husband had been healed completely of cancer. So, I began to pray and ask God how do you warn a person about what is soon going to happen and not cause

Vibratory Experiences

them to think that you are a negative person when it comes to healing. She knew I was a witness for God and God had healed me of cancer. I didn't know where to begin the conversation of telling her not to go to work next week. She needed to spend more time with her husband and pay more attention to him.

Everything I said to Anna, she countered it with, "Bill is fine and he's okay with being home alone." Again, I tried explaining to her the importance of spending quality time with her spouse. Anna said, "LaVerne, you don't understand. My husband is doing fine."

Well, I tried to prepare Anna for what was coming sooner than she thought, but it was very hard trying to convey this message to Anna. She had no idea how sick he really was. She was in denial. While sitting next to her, I could feel that Anna's chest was heavy, drowning in water (tears) and then it came through in words, "you must release the water or you will drown in pity. Stop holding on to air and feel the wind blow, release and let go."

I left the salon doubting myself and wondering if I should have said anything more to Anna.

Bill made his transition a few days after my hair appointment. A week after the funeral, I got a phone call from Anna, she admitted that she hadn't listened to me, but she was grateful that I had tried to help prepare her for her husband's death, and that meant a lot to her. God always warns us. We must believe and never doubt Him.

> "To appoint unto them that mourn in Zion,
> to give unto them beauty for ashes,
> the oil of joy for mourning,
> the garment of praise for the spirit of heaviness;
> that they might be called trees of righteousness,
> the planting of the
> Lord, that he might be glorified"
> (Isaiah 61:3).

Special Delivery

It was the day before Christmas and none of the grandchildren were going to join my husband and I for the holiday.

While cooking breakfast, I said to my husband, "It would be nice if we received at least a picture from one of the grands for Christmas." It wasn't five minutes later that the doorbell rang and it was a UPS box. It was a talking photo of one of the grandchildren.

My husband asked me, "How did you know that gift was coming?" I told him I didn't, it was a shock to me as well. I guess I placed an order into the universe.

Sadness in the Nail Salon

While sitting in the chair getting my nails done, suddenly, I felt a sadness come over me. So, I began telling myself, as usual, not to say anything because this person did not know me and might become frightened.

I decided to engage in a conversation with her anyway. She confirmed that she was sad because her fiancée was killed in a plane crash recently. I was visiting Michigan last year and the same lady walked past me in the nail salon and I felt she was pregnant. While her mom was giving me a manicure, I asked her mom if her daughter was having a baby. Her mom said, "Oh no!" I went back eight months later and the baby was due the following month. Oh well!

Who's Calling

I received a telephone call from my cousin one Sunday morning. When I picked up the telephone, I knew who it was and I said, "Hey, how are you?"

She said, "How nice it is to have caller ID."

I said, "Yes it is, let me call you back. I'm on my way to church." So, immediately the thought came to my mind, mention something about caller ID in Spilling the Beans on Jesus. It was ironic when I got to church (Mount Calvary Missionary Baptist Church of Stuart, Florida); the minister's sermon was entitled "Caller ID."

The minister talked about how God's telephone line is never busy and He does not check to see whose calling.

God never fails to answer our calls.

The Church Seat that was Left for Me

While at church (Greater Grace Temple, in Detroit) one Sunday, I sat next to a women who "I thought" had a serious attitude problem. Every time Bishop David L. Ellis (now deceased) would say, tell the one sitting next to you this or that, the lady sitting next to me would just sit there, with a frown on her face, without responding. I began to have this strange feeling in my left arm and I said, "Okay, God what is going on now."

I was also being led by the Holy Spirit to pray for her. This was a problem, I thought to myself, "This is definitely not going to work with me saying one thing to this lady sitting next to me. On top of that, I felt I needed to touch her and I really couldn't see how I was going to do that. So, at the end of the service, the minister said to hug the one that is standing next to you and tell them that God loves them and so do you. This was my opportunity to reach out and touch her. We turned to one another and hugged and that's when I began to pray for her. I told her that I had discerned that something was wrong with her arm and she said, "Yes! I just had a mastectomy due to cancer and my arm is in pain." I knew I had picked up her pain because my shoulder was in pain. Thank God that I had the opportunity to pray for her. What a RELIEF...

Ye have not chosen me,
but I have chosen you and ordained you,
that ye should go and bring forth fruit,
and that your fruit should remain:
that whosoever ye shall ask of the Father in my name,
he may give it you"
(John 15:16).

Vibratory Experiences

Presentational Encounter...

History was made with the election of Barack Obama. Prior to the election, Maria Shiver (at that time Arnold Schwarzenegger's wife), was featured on the Oprah Winfrey show. Oprah asked her, "Who do you feel is going to be upset the night of the election in your house?"

Maria said, "Arnold, because Obama is going to win." At this point, although I was praying for Obama to win, I had not received any type of confirmation, spiritual or otherwise that he would. A few days later, early in the morning I was in my sanctuary (bathroom and BAM—all at once I was getting ready to speak Obama's name to my sister and goose bumps went all over my body. At that moment I knew he had won the race. Every time I would talk about Obama, from that point on, I would get the same feeling and that was my confirmation. Thank God for showing up again.

5

Dreams

*God often reveals to me answers to issues and problem individuals are facing through dreams.
Often I have no prior knowledge of these situations.
I just get up in the morning and give them a call and tell them I had a dream about them.
The first question they always ask is,
"How did you know that I was having these problems?"*

I tell them, "I can't explain it, It's another God Encounter."

Joanne and the White House

Years ago, while dating, I had a dream after being in the presence of my male friend. When I saw him the following day, I told him that I had a dream about a lady named Joanne. He gave me this strange look and asked who is Joanne? I told him I recall having a playmate named Joanne. Well, a few weeks later when he decided to visit, I had another dream. This time, I saw him going into this white house with clothes thrown over his arm.

Months later, I found out that he was dating a woman named Joanne, and she lived in a white house. He could not figure out how I knew these things. At the time, I was young and didn't realize that God was dealing with me through dreams.

He Shall Be Healed

I woke up early one Sunday morning, after having a dream about Mr. Andrew, who was a patient at the doctor's office where I was employed. I laid in bed several minutes thinking about the dream.

In the dream, I saw Mr. Andrew in the Cardiac Car Unit. He was hooked up to several machines and had two nurses in the room with him. I walked into the room and spoke to him and the nurses. He, however, was very ill and could not respond, so I turned my attention to the nurses.

Dreams

One nurse said to the patient, I can sing you a song," and the other nurse said, "I can recite you a poem." I said, "I can't sing you a song or recite a poem, but I can pray for you, lay hands on you and you shall be healed." So, that's what I did.

When I actually woke up out of the dream, I could not rest until I found out if Mr. Andrew was really in the hospital. I knew what hospital the doctor admitted his patients to, so I called the hospital and asked the operator if they had a patient by the name of A. Andrew and the operator referred me to the Cardiac Care Unit.

The nurse told me that Mr. Andrew was there, but he was being transferred to a regular room, because he had improved overnight.

Again, you must question yourself. How do these things happen?

*"Is any sick among you?
Let him call for the elders of the church;
and let them pray over him, anointing him with oil in the name of the Lord"*
(James 5:14).

One Way Connection

In March 1987, I had a dream that I was at a funeral and everyone there was dressed in pastel colors (indicating if something was going to happen it probably would take place during the season people wore bright colors). I asked myself, "Why am I here viewing the deceased and I don't know this person?"

When I was coming out of the dream, I heard this voice that said, "You no longer need a two-way connection. You only need a one-way connection." At that moment I saw the face and upper portion of my husband's body and I woke up.

I laid in the bed wondering why I had that dream. About six months later, I noticed that my husband (Mr. Moore) was losing weight and I saw streams of blood in his sputum. He denied feeling sick or tired. I decided to make an appointment with his doctor anyway.

After he saw the doctor and had several test done, it was confirmed that he had lung cancer. Immediately, after his diagnosis, the dream came back to me. You no longer need a two-way connection, you only need a one-way line. He made his transition in September 1988.

The Little Girl Was Rescued

One of my sisters and her husband had the opportunity to change the life of a foster child, named April.

She was placed with them for only two weeks to give her foster mother a break. The placement worker told them that April was very wild and acted like an animal.

They were told that if they didn't keep her locked up in her cage, she would run in circles uncontrollable. April could not talk. Therefore, you have to pay close attention to her to meet her needs. My family became attached to April, but they knew she had to return to her regular foster home.

The foster mom was a different nationality and although she had a nursing background, she had very little knowledge about how to take care of a little black girl, especially her hair. Not only was April kept in a cage all day, the foster mom cut off all of her hair and it still remained unkept. My family

Dreams

could tell that April had the potential to do better if she was given and opportunity.

Two weeks later, the social worker returned April to that terrible environment. Our hearts were broken to see April leave. I knew personally, that she was not receiving the proper care or stimulation she needed to improve.

It was months later that I had a dream that I saw April in a hospital setting surrounded by what appeared to be doctors and other professionals trying to make a decision concerning her. I appeared in the hospital room and told the doctors that I knew this little girl and I could get her the help that she needed. Then I woke up...

I called my sister and told her the dream I had about April and that she would be getting her back very soon. She said, "We will see."

A few day later, she received a telephone call from a social worker, asking her if she would consider taking April back on a permanent basis until she could be adopted. She and her husband decided to take April back, but they knew they had a lot of work before them.

April never learned how to talk, but she did learn how to communicate her basic needs and to follow simple instructions. For example, when she was hungry, she went into the kitchen and banged on the table. After she ate breakfast, she knew it was time to get her book bag and lunch pail so she could go to school. She even became a little fashion conscious. Once her hair had grown to a manageable length, she would go and get her bucket of beautiful barrettes to be placed in her hair.

After five years of dedicated and hard work, April was adopted by another family. The adopting mom pretended that she would continue to allow my sister and her husband see April. But she didn't. I'm glad that my sister and her husband had the opportunity to make a difference.

The Day

*You never know what the day is going to bring—
Sunshine or rain,
Pain or gain,
Happiness or sadness,
Cheers or tears,
Laughter or sorrow or hope for tomorrow.*

Hope

Early one morning I had a dream about a young girl who was pregnant. Her mother worked for me at the time. I went to work that morning and told her mother that I had a dream about her daughter. I told the mother I saw doctors running down the hall with her daughter on a stretcher to the delivery room and she was having a very hard time with the delivery, however, she survived.

A few weeks later the daughter actually almost died giving birth, but the mother remembered my dream and kept the faith that her daughter was going to live.

The mother told me afterwards, that I had given her hope and she had refused to accept what the doctors told her, that her daughter might not make it. Again, dreams can come true!

Dreams

A Visit After Church

I had a dream about my former husband's friend, Robert, just before he died. Coincidently (or was it), my husband died exactly one year later, from the same type of illness. In the dream, I saw Robert's granddaughter (Sharon) Being taken away from him. He loved his granddaughter very much. Whenever my husband and I would visit him, he was always holding or interacting with her in some way. In the dream, Robert, was sick and Sharon was being taken away. I was confused about this dream at first, because it didn't appear that he was seriously ill.

So, a few days after the dream, on my way home from church, I decided to stop by and visit Robert and his wife. It was unusual for me to stop by without my former husband, but I felt compelled to do so. The wife and I had become very close. I didn't want to say anything about the dream, because I wasn't sure what the dream meant. I made my visit very short, because I could tell that he was not feeling well and I began to have a strange feeling that something wasn't right. When I left the house, I knew exactly what the dream was about. He died a few days later.

Mistaken Diagnosis

Early one Sunday morning, I recalled having a dream that one of my patients in our residential program had cancer. I called the facility and asked how the patient was doing, and I was told that she had been vomiting.

This patient had been hospitalized for bulimia, based upon her symptoms. She had cognitive deficits as a result of having an aneurysm and could not express herself thoroughly. The patient told the staff that she was focused on trying to lose weight and look the way she did when she was twenty years old. Therefore, the doctors did not look for any other problems. I felt that bulimia was not the correct diagnosis.

After having the dream, I fabricated a story to get her into the doctor's office. I lied. I told the office manager that the patient needed to see the doctor immediately, because she was bleeding.

I was told to bring her in right away. Once we got there the nursing staff quickly took her to be examined by the gynecologist, who, in turn, sent her straight to the emergency room. After several tests were done, the family was told that the patient had a bowel obstruction and needed emergency surgery.

Prior to that time, the patient was in therapy for bulimia and was being monitored after each meal so that she would not go to the bathroom and try to vomit. The truth was, she had no other choice, but to try to throw up because of the blockage, just to get some relief.

Thank God for the dream. The patient did not need therapy for bulimia, she needed treatment for cancer. Unfortunately, nine months later, she died, from advanced colon cancer.

Blind

Be guided not misdirected. When God guides you, you can be blind and know that you are going in the right direction. With sight you can take the wrong road and miss what God is trying to show you. So trust God to guide you all the way and you will end up where you are supposed to be.

The Math Problems That Were Solved

In 1987, I was studying for a Real Estate exam and the math formulas were very difficult for me to grasp. In the middle of the night, God showed me how to solve the problems. I went to take the test the following day and the math problems and the whole exam was so easy that I began to doubt myself, because I was one of the first to finish the test. I passed the State Board exam and began to sell real estate part-time and became the top sales person in the office. Working as a real estate agent allowed me to do something

I enjoyed; meet new people, assist them in finding their dream homes and expand my knowledge as a professional salesperson. I thank God for that opportunity, because I needed a change from just working with the sick.

Soul Mate

Many women may think like I did, "If he can't match what I have, we will just have some fun." I thought after my husband died in 1988, I would never marry again. Then I began to live with my mate, even though I felt it was not Godly. I was always trying to hide from the church folks the fact that I was living with my friend. The church folks were very nosy.

Oftentimes, women get hung up on titles. For example, if I can hook up with someone with a prestigious title, such as a doctor, lawyer, or judge that could match my income.

I would have it made. The title may sound good and the money too, but oftentimes it comes with a price. Money and the desire for prestige can cause you to live in a compromising situation and can be miserable.

I was coming out of a dream one morning and heard these words, "if you do it my way, I will make your way right." I knew it was God talking to me. At the time I had no desire to marry my mate, because his material possessions did not match up with mine.

But, I chose to be obedient to God and we got married. It paid off in a mighty way. Don't let money or titles get in the way. God gave me favor and increase beyond my imagination and I thank God for His Word. I am happy I listened and obeyed the word of God. My husband was my coach and my best friend. Money is not everything. Peace of mind is everything. While he was alive, I lived without shame or guilt.

Dreams

The Nap I will Never Forget

December 1998, my husband and I took a bus ride with a group of friends to Chicago, Illinois to celebrate New Year's Eve and my birthday on New Year's Day.

When we arrived at the hotel, my husband and I were disappointed with its condition and appearance. We were told by the group leader that she had not been informed that the hotel was under renovation. Their group had been there several times and the accommodations were fine and the food was superb.

My tradition is to take a nap every New Year's Eve, so that I'm awake when the New Year comes in and then to celebrate my birthday, New Year's Day. Unfortunately, this time when I took my nap, I woke up hysterical from a terrible dream. I sat straight up in the hotel bed shaking and breathing very hard. My husband asked me what was wrong. I told him I just had a dream that my mother died. He said, "It was just a dream. Go back to sleep and get some rest." I knew better, because God had always warned me about things, people, and upcoming events before they happened. My mom died twenty-three days later, the day before her birthday. I wasn't aware that my mom had told one of my sisters that she would not be here for her birthday, and that Christmas would be her last. I was unaware that I had a serious illness, but before my mom died she told me, "Now you go home and take care of yourself, because you are sick and I am okay." My mother was gifted as well.

After having a good time at the New Year's Eve party we all woke up to a snowstorm that paralyzed the entire Midwest. After being told that we would probably be stuck in Chicago for about two or three days, everyone became frustrated, because they were not prepared to stay the additional days. It was so cold in the hotel with the wind blowing the snow through the cracks of the windows and doors. I had to sleep with my fur coat on for extra warmth.

Around the second day the hotel was running out of food, because they were not prepared for a big group and could not receive any deliveries. This trip turned into a nightmare. People were running out of cash and clean clothes, and everyone wanted to get back to work. There were no stores nearby that we could purchase food items from.

On the third day, the bus driver got notice from his boss that the roads were clear and it was safe to travel. The whole group was elated when we heard the good news.

I had just finished eating a mini breakfast and all at once I begin to feel sick and started throwing up. Everyone felt that the food was old, and that was the reason why I was throwing up.

Finally, we all were heading back to Detroit. My husband and I sat in the front of the bus because I did not want to make everyone else sick by constantly throwing up.

When we made it back to Detroit, everyone's car was buried in snow. We all helped one another dig our cars out. I will never forget this trip.

I believe this was the first sign of my illness.

Dreams

My Own Diagnosis—Homeostasis

In January 1999, I went to a new internist to get my yearly checkup. The nurse called my name and I followed her toward the back of the office to see the doctor. The nurse asked me to step on the scale to check my weight and that is when I first became alarmed. The scale showed I had lost ten pounds. I went into the exam room thinking maybe the exercise that I had been doing was working. The worst thought I had was that it could be a sign of cancer. I had no clue why I had a sudden weight loss, but the doctor did not seem to be overly concerned. This was my first visit with this doctor. I gave him my complete history and told him my primary concern was that I was suffering from ongoing sinus infections. The doctor's response was, "you just have very bad allergies." While putting on my clothes, the thought that kept running through my mind was, "A sudden weight loss could be serious."

My husband and I stopped on our way home to pick up lunch. Before I could complete my sandwich, I began to throw up everywhere. Immediately, my husband called the doctor's office and asked to speak to the doctor. The nurse told my husband that the doctor was busy, but she would call the pharmacy and order medication for the nausea.

The next day I made a decision to call my gastroenterologist and explain to him about the sudden weight loss. The doctor's response was "LaVerne, you are intelligent enough to know if something is wrong with you. I'll make an appointment for you to have an Endoscopy (look in your stomach) next week."

Immediately after the internist was given the results of the Endoscopy from my gastroenterologist, he called me with a devastating report. Without any real compassion or warning as to the magnitude of the purpose for his call, he said, "Mrs. Moore, I know why you have been having those symptoms, you have stomach cancer."

I could not believe what I was hearing on the telephone. Immediately I called my husband at his business and told him the bad news. Then I called my son and the rest of my family members I was crying and in shock at the same time.

I had some knowledge of cancer and at that very moment my thoughts were that I was going to die. I decided to double check with the gastroenterologist to see if the test results the internist had given me were accurate. I began my conversation by giving the doctor my name and asking him to confirm my test results. His reply was, "Yes Mrs. Moore, you have cancer and it's in stage two and it's the worst type of cancer you can have."

After crying and crying and crying, suddenly, I remembered waking up that morning with the word homeostasis on my mind. I knew then, that God was telling me something and it was relevant to the bad news.

Usually when I get a word from the Lord, I have no clue why the word is being deposited into my spirit at that particular time. I knew the meaning of homeostasis had something to do with balance in your life. So, I proceeded to read the medical definition and decided I was going to believe that God had given me that word for a reason.

I decided to do some research for myself concerning this type of cancer. Unfortunately, everything I read was so devastating that I stopped wanting to know anything else about this type of cancer. Studies showed that the average survival rate of this type of cancer was 20%.

That weekend, my husband decided that we should get out of the house and go for a ride around Belle Isle. While waiting for him to come out of the house, I decided to whisper a little prayer to God. I told God I have been in church all of my life and I needed a scripture to give me more faith I was going to make it. God directed me to Jonh 11:4, *"This sickness is not unto death but for the glory of God that the Son of God might be glorified thereby."* When I read this scripture, I knew that God had my back.

Dreams

In March 1999, the surgeon removed 70% of my stomach. It was confirmed that I had the worst type of cancer, but it was contained and had not reached any significant stage. I thank God for His Divine Intervention.

Are you prayed up for the unexpected?

Untangled

About three months later, after having surgery for stomach cancer, the doctor suggested they should remove the rest of my stomach due to complications and create a new one. I prayed and asked God to heal my problem. Well, that's exactly what He did. I had a dream and my mom was untangling fishing lines in the trunk of her old Roadmaster car. After she untangled the lines, I heard her voice, and she said, "Lou, everything is fine you don't need surgery." Thank God for using my mom from thee other side for Divine Healing through the power of the Holy Spirit.

Batting Your Way Through Life

*What ball is being pitched to you?
Is it sickness, disease, depression, fear,
despair or perhaps that ball of peace, joy or happiness?*

Let's play baseball!

The Three Little Pigs

I woke up crying one morning and felt the presences of my mom. She was telling me to tell my sister, my ex-business partner, not to worry about the business, because it was built on solid ground—like a tree planted by the rivers of water and it shall not be moved. In the dream, my mom, gave the illustration of the three little pigs' story. One house was built with straw, the other was built with wood, and one with bricks. My mom said, they will huff and puff, but they will not blow the company down. I called my sister and gave her the message and I told her no matter how the company is discriminated against, God said, that it shall stand and not be moved. I felt so strong about this, I could not stop crying while telling my sister.

Oftentimes, being self-employed and having a volatile business, you purely operate by faith. It is always encouraging to hear from someone who has comforting words or symbolic signs confirming that your business is going to survive regardless of its current state. I believe my mother wanted

Dreams

my sister to know, through this dream, not to give up when business is unstable and for her to know that "God Is the Source of Our Supply," not man.

This dream has given my sister the confidence when things are slow that the business will stand. Today, thirty years later the business is doing very well. Thanks Be To God.

Blessed is the man that trusteth in the Lord,
and whose hope the Lord is
(Jeremiah 17:7).

6
Random Acts of Kindness

If someone has enough money to live well and sees a brother or sister in need but shows no compassion—how can God's love be in that person?
1 John 3:17(NLT)

Paying It Forward

There have been times when the Lord has spoken to my mind and led me to give someone a gift, or sow a seed into someone's life through money, words of encouragement, a food basket, flowers, clothes, jewelry, or assistance with housing. I try to be open minded when a person is in need of help. No, I am not rich, or even close to it, but I enjoy helping when I can and there is a need. On several occasions I have been told that if I keep helping people I will go broke. My response to that remark was, "The more you give the more you receive. God will supply all my needs."

"You shall love the Lord your God with all your heart, and with all your soul, and with all your strength, and with all your mind. And, love your neighbor as yourself"
Luke 10:27 (NLT).

Valentine's Day Surprise

On Valentine's Day, I went to get my hair styled. After the hair stylist finished my hair, I took my checkbook out to pay her. While writing the check for fifty dollars, "something said" she needs five-hundred dollars, so I wrote the check for five-hundred dollars instead. I left it face-down on her work station, and said have a nice day. She called me on my cell phone shouting and crying. "LaVerne!!! Girl, what's up? Why did you do that? I sure needed it. Let me pay you back. Nobody has ever given me anything."

I told her, "No! You cannot pay me back." She knew I was sincere when I told her it was an act of kindness. I told her to keep giving to others and God will take care of her needs. She went on to tell me that it had been a slow period for her and she needed exactly what I had given her.

Tears Shared with the Parking Lot Attendant

Twice a week, I volunteered in the hospital surgical lounge department in Pontiac, Michigan.

I woke up with the lot attendant on my mind. I knew something was going on with her because God always warns me about the person he wants me to help. I continued to lie in bed thinking about what to do.

The Lord spoke to my mind and told me to give her one hundred dollars. I said to myself, "I don't know this person, I'm only going to give her fifty dollars."

I tried negotiating with myself and it didn't work so I gave her the hundred dollars. When I pulled into the parking lot that morning,

I had to sign my name on a clipboard for free parking, that's when I gave her the envelope with the money in it. I said "Merry Christmas!"

She started crying and told me, "God really does answer prayers."

She said, "now I can buy my son something for Christmas." She had spent all of her money on an apartment so she and her son could be reunited again. Her son had been in foster care for a year, while she was recovering from drug abuse. She was crying and so was I. This was a heart-felt moment for me. I still don't know her name.

7

Auditory

Suddenly the Lord called out,
"Samuel!"
...And Samuel replied,
"Speak, your servant is listening"
1 Samuel 3:4,10 (NLT).

Something is Going to Happen to You Today!

In August 1974, the sun was beaming in my bedroom window like never before. When I woke up, I heard the words, "something is going to happen to you today."

I looked around the room and no one was there. I got up and looked around the house and everyone was still asleep. I stayed up and did a few errands and tried calling this patient (Mrs. Brown) that I knew from the doctor's office where I worked during the day. Mrs. Brown always asked me to come to her prayer band meeting where a few women got together and prayed.

Each time I saw Mrs. Brown, she said, "Young lady, are you ready to join us women for prayer?" I always had an excuse, because I didn't want to be bothered with the little old ladies. But...this day, I was trying my best to reach Mrs. Brown, because I felt I needed prayer. I never was able to reach her. So I began to prepare for my afternoon shift in the hospital where I was an IV Tech and Assistant Lab Tech. When I got to work, I couldn't get it together. My boss asked me why wasn't my work done I told him that I felt like something was going to happen to me. His comment was, "Yes it is. You are going to be fired, if you don't get busy." I said, "It's not that kind of feeling."

As the day progressed I continued to have, "that strange feeling" that I couldn't shake.

I decided to do something I had not done in the past, which was go out to a club after work. My girlfriend had asked me to meet her at the club to help celebrate her birthday. When I got to the club, I didn't see her. As I was leaving, a nice young man asked me if I was waiting for someone, I told him yes. He asked me to join him for a drink while I was waiting for my friend. I told him I really didn't drink, but that he could order me something anyway. I recall taking one sip of the drink.

Auditory

I was tired of waiting for my friend, so I abruptly got up from the table and walked toward the door. The young man said, "Hey I didn't get your name."

I said, "oh, it's LaVerne."

He said, "Let me walk you to your car, it's too dangerous for you to walk out there by yourself."

I said, "Oh, I'm not afraid." He walked me to my car anyway.

As I approached my car and was turning off the alarm system, I heard a voice say, "This is a robbery. Don't you move."

I said, "Excuse me sir, what did you say."

When I first heard the voice I was a little nervous, but when I turned around and saw the gun in his hand, I was terrified. Suddenly, a second robber appeared out of nowhere, and started to rob the young man who had walked me to the car. The first robber was waiving his gun back and forth between me and the good guy.

I began to pray and threw my purse at the robber with the gun, hoping that, that was all he wanted and he would leave me alone. Suddenly, I felt something hit my body. I began to feel a severe burning sensation in my stomach area. I didn't realize that I have been shot until I looked down and saw blood gushing out of the front of my body. I still had on my white uniform from work and you could really see the blood coming through my lab coat.

I staggered to the building hoping to hide from the robbers. I grabbed a hold of the brick wall at the entrance and swung my body into the archway of the lounge, trying with everything in me not to fall to the ground. I felt that if I fell, I would never get up, I would die. I was determined not to fall. I was determined to live. My body started to feel very weak and blood continued to gush from the gun shot wound. I saw my whole childhood flash before me.

No one knew I had been shot, because the gun had a silencer on it. The good guy started running back toward the lounge, but when he saw the blood and realized that I had been badly hurt he began yelling, "She's been shot! She's been shots! Get some help!"

When I got in the front door of the lounge, everyone was trying to get me to lie down and I kept telling them, "No, I can't lie down! That bullet might hit my spine." At that time I wasn't aware that the bullet had done it's damage and was somewhere on the ground.

While waiting for the ambulance to arrive, I began to tell the people that God was not ready for me—I had things to do. When the police arrived, they asked me questions about how the guys looked that attacked me. I told them they were black and that's all I knew. "Now get me to the hospital!" The police said the EMS was on the way. When EMS arrived, they wanted to take me to the nearest hospital that was right down the street from where I worked, I said, "No! Take me to Sinai Hospital, where I worked. EMS drivers said no you're losing to much blood. I said " I am not going to die." So they took me to Sinai.

The hospital staff asked me for my parent's name and phone number. I told them not to call my parents, because they might have heart attacks, So they called my brother, we lived together. After surgery, my sisters were there,. They said the doctors had told them I was very, very sick and they would be able to tell the family more about my condition in a few days. My sisters said that when I woke up after surgery and I told them that God had given me an answer that I was going to make it, but I was going to have a hard time.

They said to one another, "You know LaVerne has always had a lot of faith in God, so if she believes she is going to make it, we believe she is." I was not aware that I had said that to them. I wasn't sure how much damage the bullet had done to my body, I just knew that I was in the intensive care unit and I was very sick and was hooked up to several machines.

Auditory

The doctor explained to me in detail exactly what happened to me. As a result of the gunshot, I had 14 perforations to the abdominal area. The bullet had entered my back, ripped the tip of my kidney off and then traveled to the front and tore my insides apart. Miracles happened every day while I was in the hospital. Thank God for sparing my life.

The Enemy

The enemy is a bullet that will try to take you out.
When they missed, God took the hit.
They will try and try again and God will save you.

Divorce the Business

In 1988, my sister and I gave birth to a business. We worked together until I was diagnosed with cancer in 1999. At that time, I could no longer fulfill my responsibility and that was causing some problems, so it seemed we needed to separate.

After praying about the decision, whether to stay in the business or let go of it, God gave me an answer, He said, "Divorce the business."

I could not believe what I heard. I lay there looking around the room and I said, "Divorce my husband?"

God's response was, "No! Divorce the business."

This was not an easy thing to do, because I had put my whole heart and life into this business. I struggled with letting go. I had many restless days. I went through anger, disappointment, and a feeling of despair. I questioned. Why is this happening at this time in my life? I didn't understand everything that was going on at the time, but I knew that God was ordering my steps. I still miss the patients, but not the sleepless nights and all the drama that comes with being in business. As long as the business still exists, I will continue to pray daily that God be with my sister and that the business will continue to thrive.

Auditory

Around the Corner

When life gets you down,
Pick up the pieces and start all over again.
Don't be defeated.
See what life has for you around the corner.
It could be what you are looking for.
It you stop, you won't know.

8

Inspired Writing

"My heart is inditing a good matter: I speak of the things which I have made touching the king: my tongue is the pen of a ready writer"
Psalm 45:1 (NLT).

A Mom's Message to Her Child

A few years ago, my girlfriend's daughter Carol died suddenly. She went to bed and did not wake up the next morning. Shortly after her death, Carol came to me in a dream and was telling me what to tell her daughter, Sharon.

I felt it was too soon after the funeral to bring up the subject. I was reluctant to call her.

Sharon was the only child and was away at college when her mother died. She had the support of her father, grandmother, other close relatives and friends to help her through the lost. However, not telling her about the dream was bothering me so much that I decided to give Sharon a call. She did not know me that well, but she knew I was a close friend of her grandparents.

So, the conversations went like this, "Hi Sharon, this is your grandmother's friend, LaVerne who lives in Florida. How are you doing today?"

She said, "Okay." I told her that I had a dream about her mother a few days ago, and this conversation might be a little strange to her, but in the dream her mother wanted me to tell her a few things.

"First of all," your mother said, "Sharon don't be no fool girl, and stay in school. Don't let anyone take advantage of you." Sharon started laughing. "Those were the exact words that my mom would say to me when she was living. Thanks a lot for the information and I'm going to do what she wants me to do. Stay in school and watch my spending."

Two years later, Sharon's grandmother died suddenly. Sharon finished college and became successfully employed.

Let the Rain Fall

Step back and let the rain fall.
While our lives are being put together again,
We say, "Rain, rain go way, come back another day." That's
okay, because the rain is coming another day. But..prepare
for the sunshine that follows the rain.

Celebrating Life

I received a brochure in the mail, which gave me a list of different titles of retreats being offered by Unity Village in Missouri. I had always wanted to attend a spiritual retreat, so I called my cousin and asked her to go with me, she agreed.

I selected the retreat entitled, "Celebrating Life."

We arrived on a Saturday evening the day before Easter Sunday in 2002. While sitting in the sanctuary Easter Sunday morning, my mind began to drift away from the word of the speaker. There was a lady about four rows in front of me. I could only see the back of her head, but I began to write a letter to her.

After service was over, I went to the lobby area where coffee and donuts were being served. I began looking through the crowd trying to spot the lady I had written the letter to. Finally, I eased up to her and introduced myself and said to her, "I don't know you and you don't know me, but I was inspired to give you this letter and I feel that it's going to help you."

She looked at me rather strangely and reached for the letter. As she began to read the letter she started crying, so I asked her if she was okay and she began to cry even more. She look at me and said, "Now I know why I had to come to this retreat, it was to meet you. I guess I can go home now, because you have answered all of my questions concerning my life. Now I can return to New Jersey, and start my life over again."

I would like my readers to know that when you are inspired to tell or write someone a note in church or wherever you might be, it's difficult to recall the contents of the letter or accurately repeat what was said. I gave the letter to the person. I only know that she was pleased and said that I had answered her questions concerning the problems that she was experiencing.

A Message to My Lovely Wife

A friend of the family died after being in an automobile accident. I attended the funeral with my husband to pay respect to the family. I did not know the wife or family very well. However, about a week after the funeral I awakened about 4:00am in the morning and the deceased man (Bob) began telling me different things to tell his wife (Joyce). I was so tired, I tried to go back to sleep, but I couldn't. I was confused, because this was someone that I barely knew.

I was thinking to myself, "Why would this man interrupt me from sleeping to tell his wife something?" He was pouring information into me so fast, I got up and got a pencil and note pad. I began to write down the information and had no clue how this information was flowing through my mind so quickly. I went back to bed and tried to go to sleep again, but still I couldn't.

I walked around the house thinking, this is one encounter I am going to keep to myself. If I mention this to my husband he is going to say, "LaVerne don't call my friend with this nonsense. Wherever you are getting your information from, please ask them to give you six digits, so I can hit the lottery."

My response to him is always the same, "It doesn't work that way. I don't control the information that comes to me." I went searching the house for my husband's telephone book. Finally, I found the telephone book and copied down the telephone number, so I could give Joyce a call. For several hours I tried to avoid calling her, because I didn't feel comfortable and didn't know if she would receive what I was going to tell her. I was experiencing this heaviness in my chest and stomach area. I just needed relief. I got up enough nerve to call Joyce and she did not pick up the phone. All at once I had this feeling of relief.

Since she was not home, I could wait to make the decision whether or not to tell her about my encounter with inspirational writing—I had time to wait until she called back. Then, the phone rang. I looked at the caller ID and it was Joyce. I answered and she asked if someone called her from my number and I said yes.

In the meantime, I began to whisper a prayer to God asking him for strength to help me deliver this message to her. When I began to give her the information from her deceased husband, she began to cry and said, "He wrote me letters all the time and he would start them off saying the same thing you are saying."

He would start his letters with, "Hey girl you know that I love you. You are my best friend." Joyce said, "Those were his exact words." So she knew this had to have come from her husband, not something I was making up. He said, "I want to be missed, but don't miss me, I am fine. Take good care of the grandchildren, don't weep anymore, things will be okay. When you look at the sun, I'll be there, and when the moon reflects, I'm there too. When the trees blow, I'm there too. I am all around you. I am everywhere. Just feel my presence and laugh. Oops, that's me up to one of my tricks. Girl don't worry, I'm okay." Then Bob had a word concerning his children. None of my boys can be me, but they can surely try. Boys, look out for your mom and I will be looking out for you. My death changed my daughter that is a doctor. Now she has a different understanding about death." He went on to say, "I want to be there, but I'm needed here. I am here taking care of you. I am okay. Let me go so you can be free."

I was so relieved when Joyce said she was so happy that I called with comforting words, because she could relate to everything I told her. She commented, "I thought that I could no longer go on without him." I said to her, "Well this is what he told me about that." Then she would make another comment, and I would refer to the letter again and again. Finally, she said, "It's very strange he came to you, but I am so glad he did. I feel that I can make it now. Thanks very much for calling, call me anytime."

Listen

I will listen when rain drops fall on my roof top,
I will listen.
I will listen when the wind blows,
I will listen.
I will listen when the birds whistle for I know you,
are present and near.
I will listen and know that you are here.

Missionary in Disguise

One morning when I went to the bathroom, I heard these words, "You are my missionary in disguise." I stopped what I was doing and I heard the same thing again. "You are my missionary in disguise." Words then started coming so fast I picked up a pen and began to write and as I wrote, I cried.

I have been repeating the same prayer daily for so long. I'd pray, "Thank you, God for waking me up to see another day. Lord, give me a clear vision and understanding of my purpose here on earth and open my heart and mind so that I may receive Your purpose and plans for my life. Lord, give me a forgiving spirit..." Well, I asked and I received. When I began to hear these words, I knew God was trying to get my attention again. In tears as God inspired me to write, the following words flowed from me:

- You have given to the needy
- You have fed the hungry
- You have clothed the naked
- You have assisted in providing housing
- You have given money when I have directed you to
- You have prayed for the sick without ceasing
- You did not forsake my seniors or the helpless
- You provided them with love, care, and transportation

While writing this, I was crying and choking up with a feeling of fullness in my chest. When the words stopped coming, I realized that I was fulfilling my purpose and that God was pleased with me and it wasn't necessary for me to wear a name tag or initials behind my name saying LaVerne Moore-Slaughter—"Missionary." I knew without a shadow of a doubt that I was not man's missionary, but I was God's Missionary in Disguise.

For I was an hungred, and ye gave me meat:
I was thirsty, and ye gave me drink: I was a stranger,
and ye took me in: Naked, and ye clothed me:
I was sick, and ye visited me: I was in prison,
and ye came unto me. Then shall the righteous answer him,
saying, Lord, when saw we thee an hungred,
and fed thee? or thirsty, and gave thee drink?
When saw we thee a stranger, and took thee in? or naked,
and clothed thee? Or when saw we thee sick,
or in prison, and came unto thee?
(Matthew 25:35-39)

9

Poetry in The Moment

*That I may publish with the voice of thanksgiving,
and tell all thy wondrous works*
(Psalm 26:7).

The Power of Water

*We can feel it, touch it, see it.
Water is powerful. It can get us from point A to point B.
Water can be clear, blue and soothing.
Water can be muddy and that's when our lives are
suffering from deep within and we see nothing but
our own shadows coming back at us like the rising tide.
Try seeing through the puddles and know God is working it out.*

The Bond

*The bond that we have...What about this bond?
This bond is thick made with glue and the tear and the wear
of the bond is being stretched and
stretched like a rubber band.
Some rubber bands are thick and some are thin, but both
of them can separate through the tugging of war.
The bond is so strong something has to melt it down...
That's the enemy.
Let no man come between what God has put together.
Where two or more stand together, peace will abide.*

Don't Stop

*Don't stop, when worrying tries to get you down.
Don't stop, it's time to go forward.
To see what life has for you.
If you stop now, you will never know.*

Being Stuck

Being stuck...you can't go forward or backwards.
Can I get unstuck? Yes!
While being stuck, know that I am God
and I will release you.
Your mind can keep you stuck.
Trust in God with your mind, body and soul.
Know that God can do all things.

White Feather

Fly light in the winds like a feather.
Just don't blow away.
Cry like a river that overflows with water.
Just don't drown.

W's

Wonder what the world would be like if we would face
the truth and not tolerate what appears
to be acceptable.
Especially when we know better.
Why do we put up with things that make us feel bad
or uncomfortable?
God knows all about it.
Why not let God have His way.

Windows

*Looking out of the window, Some windows are clear,
Some are smudge,
Some are tinted.
What would you see if you looked out of yours?*

Light

*I can see the light, the light that shines from within,
The light that surrounds me from day to day,
The light that goes forward to direct my path.
The light is Jesus and He helps me find the way.*

Joy

*When the joy of life begins, you will forget about yesterdays'
sorrows and begin a new day.
This new day will carry you through, until you are
overflowing with the joy within again.*

Anger

*Release anger, Release pain and gain.
Don't be trapped by anger.*

Peace

*I demand peace, love and joy.
Through peace I can treat others the way I want to
be treated. Through joy, I can express and spread my joy
throughout the world. Through love that
lifted me, I can share it with others. I go deep within my
being and find just what I need, and
that's the peace that surpasses all understanding.
Peace to deal with every problem that I'm faced with. It no
longer remains a problem, it just melts way.*

*Peace I leave with you; my peace I give you.
I do not give to you as the world gives.
Do not let your hearts be troubled and do not be afraid
(John 14:27).*

Rise Up

*Don't let bad thoughts weigh you down.
Rise up like the sun that rises every day.
Sometimes when we look outside the sun is hidden
behind the clouds, like our problems are.
Rise up anyway, face the problem and let it go.
Start over tomorrow and deal with the rise.*

A Mirror

*A mirror is a reflection of you—
Your past and your future. What you see is what you get.
We are who we see in the mirror, Good or bad.*

God Bless the Child Who has His Own

The pennies from heaven. Keep a penny just for you.
Keep a penny.
Now share the penny.
Do you really want your penny?
Yes!
If yes, that's okay.
God wants us to depend on Him, not man, for our penny.
Man will let you down.
Trust God for your penny and everything else.

Poetry in the Moment

The War of the Family
The family war is a chemical warfare, When they spray and spread rumors and cause you to take cover,
You will run You will hide
You will flee from the enemy.
God wants peace, not war.
The joy of the Lord is my strength (Nehemiah 8:10).
Be a winner in the midst of war.
Know that God will see you through.
Be prepared for battle in your life; know it is all good for those who know the Lord.
We are in a war zone (the world).

No one knows the extend of the zone,
No one knows how far and to what extent the war will be, but trust God and know that God will give you victory.
It's not about who wins, it's about who finished the course with integrity and dignity;

Poetry in The Moment

Not who throws the mud the farthest,
but who stood in the mud.
Remember, we are soldiers in the army. We must fight no
matter how hard it is. We must hold up the blood,
stained banner and be free...
Let freedom ring... Let freedom ring...

"You will not have to fight this battle.
Take up your positions; stand firm and see the deliverance of
the LORD will give you, O Judah and Jerusalem.
Do not be afraid; do not be discouraged.
God out to face them tomorrow,
and the LORD will be with you"
(2 Chronicles 20:17 NIV).

10

My Definitions

"The fear of the LORD is the beginning of wisdom; a good understanding have all they that do His commandments; His praise endureth for ever"
(Psalm 111:10).

The Way I Define Certain Words

Many of the words in this book you may not have ever heard of before or used in the way I chose to use them, therefore, I am including for your information definitions of certain words based on their usage in this book.

Automatic Writing: you are inspired to write without the knowledge of knowing why.

Auditory: When you hear the voice of the Lord (or some people might say spirit) talking to you.

Alternative Medicine: Using alternative medicine is not discrediting the traditional medicine usage. It gives you a choice. Alternative medicine can be used in conjunction with your traditional medicine, but you are advised to inform your doctor if you are taking remedies or using homeopathic methods. I personally feel getting massages or reflexology and seeing a chiropractor that is in tune with you will give you a sense of balance and enhance your overall well-being.

Discernment: Being able to discern is a gift from God. As an individual you are able to see through people that are real or phony. Personally, I have been led to help people who are in need just by being in their presence and having the ability to look at them and know that they had a problem. With the natural eye they look normal, but with the spiritual eye you see something different. In some cases you can discern if the person is sick or if they are a drug user or something simply is just not right about the person. You are able to look at the person and know if this is someone who is trustworthy or not. At times, having this gift can cause you to be judgmental and that's not always a good thing.

My Definitions

Intuition: Having a feeling of knowing things without conscious reasoning.

Vibratory: Being able to sense or pick up a person's vibration.

Vision: Being between asleep and awake.

Epilogue

Understanding the interpretation of feelings are entirely your own. With this in mind, what you see, what you feel, what you believe may not be the same as what someone else might or might not believe. However, in my world, my existence, *encounters with God are real*.

About the Author

LaVerne Moore-Slaughter was born and raised in Detroit, Michigan, in a caring and stable environment. The focus in the family at the time was working hard and not hugs and kisses.

LaVerne has been involved in several business endeavors, but enjoyed the healthcare business the most. Her passion was advocating and caring for the sick.

As a goal oriented person, she believes in positive thinking, daily prayer, and affirmations. At an early age, she recalls seeing the image of God in the mirror of her old fashioned dresser. At first, this was scary to her. As she matured spiritually, she began to have different experiences which she refers to as God Encounters. She no longer tries to understand or explain why she has these feelings. She realizes and is grateful, that God uses her to encourage, inspire, and uplift and edify His people by giving her messages to share with them through dreams, visions, vibratory experiences, spiritual discernment, auditory encounters and inspired writings.

Normally, these feelings come while she is in the presence of an individual, church, at work, or even in the salon. LaVerne also has received messages for others while in the shower or while standing at the kitchen sink, It is never planned or premeditated, it just happens...

In February 1999, Laverne went to the doctor for a sinus infection and later found out she had stomach cancer. After the shocking news of cancer, she decided to divorce the rehab business and move to Florida with her then husband. There, she has been able to focus on living a stress-free life and having an attitude of gratitude.

To order additional copies of *God Encounters are Real*, or to find out more about Laverne Moore-Slaughter please visit www.encountersarereal.net.

A portion of all proceeds from the sell of this book will be used to support life affirming non-profit organizations.